Russian Economic Reforms as Seen by an Insider

Success or Failure?

Vladimir Mau

THE ROYAL INSTITUTE OF
INTERNATIONAL AFFAIRS
International Economics Programme

Published in Great Britain in 2000
by the Royal Institute of International Affairs,
Chatham House, 10 St James's Square, London SW1Y 4LE (Charity
Registration No. 208 223)

Distributed worldwide by the Brookings Institution,
1775 Massachusetts Avenue, NW, Washington, DC 20036-2188

ISBN 1 86203 108 8

Cover design by Matthew Link
Printed and bound in Great Britain by the Chameleon Press Ltd

*The Royal Institute of International Affairs is an independent body which
promotes the rigorous study of international questions and does not express
opinions of its own. The opinions expressed in this publication are the
responsibility of the author.*

CONTENTS

FOREWORD

Few countries can have been more misunderstood than post-Soviet Russia, particularly in its struggle to build a market economy on the ruins of central planning. The basic reason for Western misperceptions is not hard to find: before 1991 specialist knowledge of Russia was concentrated among Sovietologists, who rarely had any training in economics.

Before 1991 knowledge of economics had been irrelevant, but now it became central. Economists, as a rule, had minimal knowledge or understanding of the Soviet system and of central planning. As a result they were incapable, despite their technical skills, either of understanding the many problems which the Russian 'transition' has encountered or of appreciating the importance and scale of the economic achievements in the teeth of those problems. For example, Professor Stiglitz, whose strictures are subjected to a powerful critique by Vladimir Mau, has expressed astonishment that in the 1990s Russia simultaneously experienced an unprecedented recession and an unprecedented growth of inequality. This may defy the laws of economic science, but there is no mystery here for anyone with an understanding of the way Soviet central planning functioned, not to mention the social and ethical wasteland bequeathed by the Soviet system.

Misperceptions have also been rife on a more superficial level. Western media coverage of Russian reform has tended to hold reform and the reformers primarily responsible for all the setbacks and hardships, as opposed to the 'torment and ulcers' (in Solzhenitsyn's words) which reform had to try to cure, or at least overcome. The standard Western tone has been one of censorious moralizing, with lashings of hypocrisy, as in the recent condemnation of Russia's military action in Chechnya. This perspective has, on occasion, given way to the opposite extreme of euphoria, as during the great foreign financial speculation in Russia in 1997.

Lucid and rigorous analysis has frequently been stifled. It is this precious commodity that Vladimir Mau provides in this paper. In the face of the wave of wise-after-the-event criticism of Russian economic reform, he demonstrates how narrow was the reformers' room for manoeuvre, and how much worse were the alternatives. The central argument is complemented by a *sottisier* of fashionable nostrums such as the neglected merits for Russia of the Chinese model.

I am not only grateful but also honoured that Vladimir Mau has chosen to publish this paper with the *International Economics Programme of the Royal Institute of International Affairs*. There are few things more alarming than conventional wisdom, which I hope will be healthily disturbed by Vladimir Mau's analysis.

Dr Brigitte Granville
Head, International Economics Programme
Royal Institute of International Affairs

ABOUT THE AUTHOR

Professor Vladimir A. Mau is Director of the Russian government's Working Centre for Economic Reform, and Deputy Director of the Institute for the Economy in Transition, where he heads the Department for Political Studies of Economic Reforms. He is a professor at the Moscow High School of Economics, a full member of the Russian Academy of Natural Sciences, and a member of the editorial board of a number of journals including *Voprosy Ekonomiki*. He has published widely in both English and Russian across the field of political economy, including *The Political History of Economic Reform in Russia, 1985–1994* (1996), *Economy and Law* (1998), and *Economic Reform through the Prism of Constitution and Politics* (1999).

He obtained his doctorate in economic sciences from the Russian Academy of National Economy and in applied economics from the Université Pierre Mendès-France, Grenoble. He has held several government and other political advisory posts, and a fellowship at Christ Church, Oxford.

ACKNOWLEDGMENTS

I should like to thank Brigitte Granville (RIIA), Yegor Gaidar (Institute for the Economy in Transition, IET), Kate Mortimer (Know-How Fund), Marcelo Selowsky (IBRD), Irina Starodubrovskaya (Foundation for Enterprise Restructuring), Pekka Sutela (Bank of Finland Institute for Economies in Transition, BOFIT), Ivan Szegvari (EBRD) and Haim Zaltzman (Stanford University, who helped in editing the English translation) for their support and encouragement. I am grateful to Joseph Stiglitz, with whom I had an important discussion on these issues at the Nobel Symposium at Stockholm in September 1999. I am also grateful for editorial work on the text to Sarah Smith and Margaret May of the RIIA publications department, and for bibliographic assistance from Mary Bone of the Chatham House Library.

February 2000   V.M.

SUMMARY

In the late 1990s the results of the Russian economic transition appeared to be quite different from those in the countries of central and eastern Europe. Consequently, the initial strong and unreserved admiration for the peaceful and unexpected collapse of the Soviet system gave way to equally strong and unreserved criticism. This paper discusses the results of the Russian reforms and the main arguments of Western critics.

The analysis is based primarily on the arguments of Joseph Stiglitz's *Whither Reform?* – a paper that contains a representative and reasoned set of 'accusations' against Russian reforms. Vladimir Mau does not seek to justify all the results of the Russian transformation. Nor does he assert that there were no mistakes or serious problems. His main aim is to analyse the real trends and the real alternatives in the transition, which differed radically from the simplified models of Western critics.

Four main aspects of Western criticism are considered: (1) whether Russian reformers could have followed the Chinese pattern; (2) the role of financial stabilization and its relationship to institutional reforms; (3) the specifics of Russian privatization; and (4) the role of Western recommendations and advisers in the post-communist reforms. The author demonstrates that most of this criticism results from a lack of knowledge by Western analysts of important details of the Russian transformation.

Unlike most of the other Eastern-bloc countries, Russia has had to overcome its own social and economic system, not a regime that had been imposed from abroad. In a divided society, a weak government found it hard to control the political and economic processes of transition. The paper argues that this transformation is a real revolution, comparable to the great European revolutions of the past. Such an approach contributes to a better understanding of contemporary developments in Russia, including macroeconomics, institutional reforms, the role of the oligarchy and privatization.

'If you can trust yourself when all men doubt you,
But make allowance for their doubting too…'
– RUDYARD KIPLING, *If*

'It was the best of times,
it was the worst of times,
it was the age of wisdom,
it was the age of foolishness,
it was the epoch of belief,
it was the epoch of incredulity,
it was the season of Light,
it was the season of Darkness,
it was the spring of hope,
it was the winter of despair,
we had everything before us,
we had nothing before us,
we were all going direct to Heaven,
we were all going direct the other way.'
– CHARLES DICKENS, *A Tale of Two Cities*

1 INTRODUCTION

To censure the result of Russian economic reform has become as fashionable as criticizing fatty food or fighting cholesterol. In fact, opposing Russian reform is now a popular trend, and any attempt to justify or explain the events in Russia or to underline Russian achievements falls on deaf ears. My own experience shows that offering a balanced, non-emotional analysis of events in 1990s Russia only results in my listeners' confusion and incredulity followed by sneering questions like 'We thought that the oligarchs had robbed the country?'. (In similar fashion, in Stalin's USSR any positive example of American life was proudly met with the retort – 'Yes, but they lynch blacks, don't they?'.)

It goes without saying that Russian reform cannot be assessed as very successful. However, it is important that the reform programme be thoroughly assessed and professionally analysed without bias. This analysis differs radically from today's typical political statements, or pseudo-academic rhetoric, where the knowledge of real facts and events is replaced by a deep (or not very deep) knowledge of theory.

Among recent publications J. Stiglitz's *Whither Reform?* (Stiglitz, 1999) and a number of pieces in the magazine *Transition*[1] have perpetuated this negative viewpoint. The

[1] The June 1999 issue of *Transition* is the most vivid example. In

fact that Stiglitz is a world-renowned economist whose books are widely read makes the situation even worse. *Transition* was very popular among Russian reformers in the first half of the 1990s; since then it has joined a long list of criticism-oriented publications.

Fashion matters, and the current trend is to see Russia's situation as bleak: any change, it seems, can only be for the worse. But trends, if left unexamined, can easily become absurd. For example, the following extract was culled from R. Rose's study on public opinion surveys, published in spring 1999:

> The New Russian Economic Barometer survey found that in early spring 1998, three out of five Russians routinely did not receive the wages or pension to which they were entitled; this number has *certainly* increased since the financial collapse of last August [1998]. (Rose, 1999, p. 9; my italics)

This type of *post factum* forecast reflects a belief that no other scenario is suitable for Russia – things can *certainly* change only from bad to worse. However, available statistical data illustrate quite the opposite: after the crisis and, probably, owing to the crisis, arrears on wages and pensions payments have been decreasing rapidly.

In the first part of this paper, I briefly discuss and comment on a number of the most widespread criticisms of Russian reforms and Russian reformers. In the second part, I point out significant peculiarities of

particular, articles by R. Rose, T. Morita and V. Brovkin illustrate the impact fashionable trends and common wisdom make on the most responsible and 'politically correct' representatives of the international economic community.-

Russia's post-communist transformation that Western economists have not taken into consideration. Space restrictions mean I cannot analyse every reproach or list every alternative point of view. I hope that readers will consult studies that examine the appropriate issues in detail. The fact that many publications denigrating Russia's experience lack information regarding Russian reforms makes this exercise a crucial one.

There are many theories as to why Russian reforms were not successful, and many reasons to blame Russian reformers. I will start with a discussion of the most significant ones.

2 THE FAILURE OF RUSSIAN ECONOMIC REFORMS

The Chinese experience has been ignored

Initially, the idea that Russia had failed to learn from the Chinese experience was mostly raised by those among the traditional Soviet *nomenklatura* (elite) who supported a moderate drive for reform. Today, this theory is becoming more and more popular among Western economists.[2]

Critics in the *nomenklatura* could see that the Chinese path would have not only preserved but also stabilized their political and economic power, at least for another couple of decades. The most energetic advocate for the Chinese way was Arkady Volsky, nicknamed the 'Russian Deng Xiaoping' in the early 1990s. The same argument fits the rhetoric of Yevgenii Primakov, another candidate for the 'Deng' title. A theoretical justification for the Chinese thesis was also stressed by the members of the economic section of the Russian Academy of Sciences. Many of these critics (such as academicians Leonid Abalkin, Oleg Bogomolov and Dmitrii Lvov) were the founders of Gorbachev's reforms.

The Chinese way entails leaving power in the hands of an old *nomenklatura* in order to preserve a one-party system and the ideological purity of a regime. Economic transformations, then, are to be undertaken gradually,

[2] See, for example, Intrilligator, 1996.

under the *nomenklatura*'s control. Any attempt to increase the political activity of individual representatives must be suppressed.

It is troubling that Western economists, who have been brought up in the tradition of political democracy and political correctness, regret that the Chinese experience was not used.[3] There are several reasons why, from both an economic and a socio-political perspective, the Chinese experience is not applicable to modern Russia.

Politically, China's experience is irrelevant to post-communist Russia. Key to the Chinese model is the existence of a totalitarian regime capable of controlling the country through its party and its intelligence services. The liberal reforms that began in Russia in 1991–2 were launched at a time when not only was there no strong state, there was no state at all. The USSR had been already dissolved, and Russian sovereignty existed only on paper.

Perhaps all responsibility for ignoring the Chinese experience should be laid at the door of Mikhail Gorbachev and his prime minister, Nikolai Ryzhkov, as well as the domestic advocates of this 'Chinese' programme (most of them were integrated into the party and Soviet elite and were directly involved in the strategic planning of the economic development of the USSR). However, such reproaches are groundless: the social and economic

[3] Intrilligator was one of the first well-known Western economists (excluding so-called Sovietologists) to advocate the application of the Chinese experience to Russia. A corresponding system of arguments was presented in a report by a number of renowned Russian and American economists. See Abalkin et al. (1996).

5

conditions of the USSR in the 1980s were dramatically different from those in China before and after its reforms.

The social and economic structure of Chinese society is similar to that of the USSR in the 1920s during the New Economic Policy (NEP) era. The ratio of urban to rural population, the GNP and employment structure, the literacy rate, the social security system and the GNP per capita all suggest a similarity between the USSR of the 1920–30s and China in the 1980–90s. Indeed, the Chinese transformation may suggest how Russia could have been industrialized during the NEP period in a 'softer' way.[4]

Three conditions are important in implementing the model of accelerated economic development while preserving a totalitarian regime. First, economic development targets should be set at a low level because a significant proportion of the labour force is not actively involved in production (i.e. there is rural overpopulation). Second, social development targets should be set at a low level (the level of the state's social responsibilities is not the same as in developed societies; for example, the Chinese social security and pension provision system covers no more than 20 per cent of its population, compared with the USSR where the system

[4] In Soviet history, the movement towards gradual industrialization, through the development of private farms and light industry, was connected with the name of Nikolai Bukharin, who proclaimed the slogan 'Get richer!' The industrialization model proposed by Bukharin was stigmatized by Stalin as 'deviation', and its advocates paid with their lives. During the following decades, the Bukharin model's viability and its compatibility with a communist totalitarian state had been an issue of theoretical discussion. China showed that the model was a real and practical economic alternative (we are not talking about politics here).

covered the whole population). Third, low cultural and educational attainment levels should be set, given that the demand for democratization is not an important issue among the bulk of the population.[5]

These factors are all present in China – and none of them existed in the Soviet Union of the 1980s. In fact, anyone who regrets that Gorbachev did not follow Deng Xiaoping's way or who recommended that Russia learn from China would have to agree with the following prerequisites for the government: first and foremost, it should reject its social responsibilities and stop paying for pensions and social benefits; second, it should cut the provision of free education and health services; and third, it should adjust the level of budget burden as a percentage of GDP from the current 35 per cent to approximately 20–25 per cent.[6] However, as far as we know, advocates of the Chinese recipe are, to a large extent, motivated by concern about the deteriorating social situation in Russia and demand its improvement. Their recommendation of the Chinese model is thus not based on a realistic economic policy but on useless dreams 'to make everything better'.[7]

[5] For more details of the interaction between the political and economic factors of Gorbachev's reforms and post-communist Russia see Gaidar (ed.) (1998), chapters 1–3.

[6] The most consistent economists stick to the same idea, taking the level of budget burden as an explanation for the drastic difference in the growth rate between communist China and post-communist Russia. See, for example, Illarionov (1998) and Aven (1999).

[7] Gorbachev was very much aware of this. I once asked him why neither he nor his colleagues had ever tried to follow the Chinese way. The president was surprised and said that everyone had already realized the principal differences between the situation in the USSR and that in China.

I do not want to get bogged down with the question of whether the initial conditions in China were more or less favourable than those in the USSR when restructuring started. Stiglitz's contention that 'China's challenges were greater, for it had to manage the challenges of transition and of development simultaneously' (Stiglitz, 1999, p. 3) is irrelevant to the Russian situation. The Soviet Union not only had to reorient its labour production towards the market, it also had to implement deep structural reform in order to transform an industrial economy into a post-industrial one. Forming new sectors of the economy, given an existing industrial system with its priorities and powerful interest groups, is no less difficult than the creation of modern industrial sectors.

The development of democracy was equally complicated. The Soviet society of the 1980s was mature and well educated, and the country was relatively open to a Western lifestyle. As a result, the population accepted the reforming initiative of the party's leadership. Because of the experiences of the 1960s (when USSR leaders rejected economic reforms and suppressed reforms in Czechoslovakia), nobody believed that the party leaders were serious. The population viewed statements about reforms as a provocation by the state security service (the KGB) to test the loyalty of the citizens. Only because the government was ready for real political change were the leaders able to introduce economic reforms; at the same time, they were able to silence the majority of party leaders who considered Gorbachev's initiatives an imprudent annoyance.

All the arguments that economic reforms should have

been undertaken before political reforms, democratic development, freedom of speech and the freeing of political prisoners are groundless. They are incorrect from a political–economic point of view and amoral to boot.[8] Any appeal to turn to the Chinese model implies strengthening the totalitarian character of society, and sparking a neo-communist reaction. On 1 July 1996, before the second round of the presidential elections, a number of well-known economists from Russia and the USA published a letter containing proposals for a Chinese version of economic reform in Russia. It is significant that many people treated this letter as a declaration of support for a candidate from the Communist Party of the Russian Federation (Abalkin et al., 1996).

The role of financial stabilization

The other criticism frequently directed at the Russian reformers focuses on their fascination with macro-economics (or, to be more accurate, with the issues of financial stabilization) rather than the implementation of institutional reforms. It has been said that 'shock therapy' devastated the population's savings and decreased consumer demand, creating, in turn, the conditions for

[8] Even so, these arguments are very popular among Western experts (especially left-leaning ones). A famous Italian economist, an expert on the USSR and Russia, was shocked when I said, in response to his reiteration of the traditional explanation for the mistakes made by Gorbachev in moving towards political reforms, that there was a historical precedent. I suggested that Italy would have avoided many of its recent problems if Mussolini had not involved the country in the Second World War but had continued in power until the 1970s. The comparison is not an inappropriate one.

a sharp decline in production and privatization distortions. In addition, there is an argument about the harmful nature of the domestic debt market that was introduced – the notorious GKO pyramid.[9] Vladimir Brovkin is typical of commentators on Russia when he writes: 'What was worse for Russian economy was the government's pursuit of a policy of macroeconomic stabilization.' (Brovkin, 1999)

The many critical voices raised against Russia sound a single note, though they are often talking about different things. The most educated and the least politically engaged economists assert that the fascination with macroeconomic stabilization has pushed aside any institutional reforms. They argue that institutional reforms were not part of the overall reform plan as they should have been; and that they also could have been undertaken with the same shock therapy methods (Stiglitz, 1999, p. 22). Others believe that macroeconomic stabilization was a mistake because it led to a sharp real appreciation of the rouble which, in turn, devastated domestic producers (Brovkin, 1999, pp 22–23). Finally, some writers are convinced of the harmful nature of a macroeconomic stabilization policy (in other words, financial stabilization, or shock therapy).[10] It is interesting that advocates of shock therapy often

[9] GKO (*gosudarstvennye kaznacheiskie obyazatelstva*) – short-term treasury bills, first issued in May 1993 – played a key role in financing the Russian budget in 1996–8. They defaulted in August 1999 and are now considered to be a symbol of 'unsustainable stabilization' – macroeconomic stabilization with a high budget deficit.

[10] See, for instance, Paul Fisher, *Transition*, June 1999, p. 34.

mention authorities such as J. Stiglitz or K. Arrow as if they had also considered a decisive stabilization policy dangerous and distracting.[11]

Several issues are muddled together here. They include the expediency of shock therapy policy, factors predetermining the transition to such a policy, mechanisms to implement macroeconomic stabilization, the ratio between macroeconomic stabilization and institutional reforms and the more general issue of the sequencing of economic reforms after the collapse of communism.

If shock therapy implies decisive and rapid macroeconomic stabilization achieving stable prices, a balanced budget and the transformation of the national currency into a tool for economic agents to perform their transactions, such a policy was only partially implemented in Russia. The most important achievement of the first phase of economic reform was that the shortage of goods was overcome, the threat of hunger in the winter of 1991–2 was avoided, and the rouble became convertible in current accounts. Such an achievement is not inconsequential in a country with a 60-year history of shortages and criminal punishment for hard-currency transactions. But it is not enough to be called shock therapy. It took four more years for the rouble to acquire some kind of stability – in 1996. It took three more years for the country to achieve at least the initial balance of

[11] Stiglitz maintains: 'I have no great quarrel with "shock therapy" as a measure to quickly reset expectations say in an anti-inflation program. The controversy was more about the attempted use of a shock therapy approach to "install" institutions – where it might more aptly be called a "blitzkrieg" approach.' See Stiglitz, 1999, p. 22.

its budget – in 1999. Altogether, it took seven years to resolve the very first tasks of macroeconomic stabilization. What a shocking therapy it was!

Shock therapy is frequently understood not as a specific, logical economic policy with set results, but as the painful consequences of macroeconomic decisions such as an increase in prices and unemployment rates, the growth of poverty and social stratification, sometimes even demographic decline.[12] Emotional writers consistently link all of these social disadvantages and problems with the liberalization and stabilization measures undertaken during the first post-communist governments. In fact, the social adjustment burden was the result of the financial crisis at the moment of entering the post-communist period, and not of the stabilization policy. In other words, the shock therapy aspect of the stabilization programme was, for the most part, predetermined by the policy of the last communist government and not by the reformers. The most unbalanced economies were in the countries of the former Soviet Union and in Poland; and it was here that shock therapy was implemented.[13]

[12] Gaidar and his colleagues were blamed for a decline in the Russian birth rate three months after they had joined the government and one month after they had started liberalization. As we can see, from the very beginning their critics believed in the supernatural power of the reformers.

[13] Polish reformers had an advantage. The last communist government, led by Mieczysław Rakowski, refused to regulate prices on many groups of goods. This decision brought hidden inflation into the open. The first post-communist government led by Tadeusz Mazowiecki and Leszek Balcerowicz needed only to finish the liberalization process and implement stabilization measures. In Russia, Gaidar had to deal with a whole range of challenges over both liberalization and stabilization.

In Hungary and Czechoslovakia, the last communist governments pursued a rather cautious financial policy. After the move away from communism, the changes in corresponding economic indicators were much more moderate. As a result, it was not so difficult to implement stabilization measures there, especially social and political measures.[14] (See Table 1.)

It was not the shock therapy programme but the refusal to stick to it that led to the many failures in Russia's post-communist development, including its institutional problems. The decline of investments, foreign businesses' lack of interest in Russian enterprises, unstable production conditions and the many defects of privatization are all associated with the long-overdue and incomplete financial stabilization processes. It was not the monetary stabilization *per se* that fuelled the dollarization of savings and transactions, the currency appreciation and the contraction of output.[15]

The main issue is not that inflation is unfavourable for investments: there are several examples of inves-

[14] The term 'shock therapy' seems to be used to describe unsuccessful attempts at stabilization. Shock therapy in Russia was seen as bad because it was inconsistent and incomplete, yet it has not been criticized in Estonia, Latvia or Lithuania, where the stabilization measures were no easier than in Russia from a social point of view. Western critics also seem reluctant to use the term to describe measures taken in Poland: the Polish experience does not fit the standard criticisms of shock therapy.

[15] See Brovkin, 1999, p. 23. This is another example of selective criticism of the stabilization policy. The situation in Russia was not too different from the situation in Estonia, where the kroon was much more closely linked to the Deutschmark than the rouble was to the dollar. However, Russian policy was more heavily criticized and generally perceived as the reason for institutional disasters.

Table 1: Budget deficit/surplus (-/+ % GDP) and inflation growth (% on previous year) before and after the onset of post-communist reforms

	1989	1990	1991	1992	1993	1994
Russia						
Budget	-8.6	-10.3	-30.9	-29.4	-9.8	-11.8
Inflation	1.9	5.0	161	2,506	840	204.4
Poland						
Budget	-7.4	3.1	-6.7	-6.7	-3.1	-3.1
Inflation	247	249	60.4	44.3	37.6	29.4
Hungary						
Budget	-0.2	-1.4	0.4	-2.9	-6.8	-5.5
Inflation	16.7	16.9	33.4	32.2	21.6	21.1
Czech Republic						
Budget	-2.8	0.1	-1.9	-3.1	0.5	-1.2
Inflation		18.4	58.3	9.1	25.1	11.7

Sources: World Bank, 1992; Gaidar, 1998, pp. 198, 218, 235; Sinel'nikov, 1995, pp. 24–25, 70.

tments and economic growth taking place while inflation approaches 100 per cent per annum. There is another and more complicated mechanism that appears to foster institutional limitations on economic activities. As Yegor Gaidar (1997) pointed out, in a post-communist country there is a clear connection between the duration of a period of high inflation and the extent of a budget crisis. The longer there is high inflation, the stronger is the addiction of the government and the economy to an inflation tax; the greater the inflation tax, the further the tax system degenerates. Thus, an incomplete (or un-realized) process of shock therapy caused the erosion of resources available to the budget, the crisis in the budget sphere and the need for internal borrowings in the form

14

of GKOs. In addition, the budget deficit spurred a strong increase in real terms in the rouble exchange rate. A stable national currency was necessary to solve the budget problems through internal borrowing mechanisms. Furthermore, the more the budget depended on the financial market the less the government could manoeuvre.

To summarize, incomplete macroeconomic stabilization and the reformers' inability to realize shock therapy measures dramatically aggravated a budget system in crisis – in terms of both expenditure and revenue. This, in turn, set in motion a deep crisis within the developing institutional structure and within the government itself.

Shock therapy is often criticized because reforms are undertaken in the wrong sequence. It is said that institutional reforms and privatization should take place first, and then liberalization and stabilization.[16] This may be correct, but the experiences of those countries that have undertaken market reforms suggests that this concept is not viable. (Sooner or later North Korea and Cuba, the last two communist countries, will have to undertake market reforms – maybe they will have different results?)

J. Stiglitz was right when he pointed out the correlation between shock therapy and institutional reforms. In fact, institution building takes a significant time and cannot use a 'blitzkrieg' methodology (Stiglitz, 1999, p. 22). However, the fact that one or other model seems

[16] The '500 days' programme created by Grigorii Yavlinsky and Stanislav Shatalin was based on this logic – privatization before liberalization. The leader of Yabloko later insisted that the given sequence of reforms was implemented.

justified theoretically does not guarantee that it can be implemented in practice. Keeping this point in mind is important in the analysis of Russian privatization.

The Russian privatization experience

The results of Russian privatization are broadly viewed as negative, although the privatization programme was seen as positive during the first years of its implementation. This failure derives from the same characteristics that everybody initially applauded: the rapid and 'massive' nature of the privatization programme in Russia.[17]

Critics have condemned the Russian privatization programme for a number of reasons. First, it was implemented too rapidly, without appropriate institutional preparation and legislation. Second, privatization weakened state power, eroded public order and fuelled corruption. Third, privatization did not create real owners of property; in fact, there was a criminal element to all (or almost all) property privatization. Voucher mechanism defects, the personal desire of the reformers to accelerate the break with communism and sometimes their dishonesty – all these arguments are used to explain why privatization did not work properly.

Now there are suggestions that the privatization process should have been undertaken gradually and in parallel with the creation of appropriate market institutions that would have secured a longer period of state

[17] For an analysis of the privatization process, see Radygin (1996) and Yegor Gaidar, ed. (1998), chapters 12 and 13.

control over property and its proper usage. Other privatization mechanisms have also been put forward; for example, privatization in favour of stakeholders or leasing mechanisms (to rent with the right to purchase). Unfortunately, none of these suggestions take into consideration the economic, political and legal situation at the beginning of the privatization process in Russia.

To move on to those 'miserable' vouchers. Gaidar, Anatoly Chubais and their colleagues were against the free distribution of property through privatization vouchers.[18] Initially, they considered a gradual privatization for cash. However, the conditions of the early 1990s dictated a different approach. In June 1991, the law on the privatization of state and municipal enterprises was adopted. This established the legal basis for privatization in Russia. It was this law that prescribed individual privatization accounts, in essence the non-cash mechanism of privatization. It soon became clear that such a system was inefficient and vulnerable to corruption. The reformers decided to cancel it. However, in the process of discussions with the legislature, the negotiators reached a compromise to keep privatization vouchers but to make them impersonal. It was impossible to consider a total rejection of non-monetary privatization mechanisms (see Radygin, 1996, pp. 78, 83).

[18] Dmitrii Vasilyev was one of the founders and advocates of voucher privatization. According to Vasilyev: 'In the beginning, our views of the privatization (Chubais's, mine and a majority of our advisers) were significantly different from the ideas realized in practice (see Radygin, 1994, p. 10). This was written before voucher privatization was completed. The author should not be blamed for changing his view as a result of later experience or criticism by his political opponents.

The speed of privatization also became a very critical issue. Nowadays, one can discuss whether it would have been more reasonable to leave the majority of enterprises as state properties and gradually perform a case-by-case privatization. But the state did not have any control over its property, which *de facto* was being controlled by management. After 1988 the process of 'spontaneous privatization' started gaining momentum. Spontaneous privatization is a euphemism for the transfer of state property into the hands of those who use it. This was initiated by the USSR law on state enterprises (30 June 1987). In accordance with that law, labour collectives (in fact, directors and managers) became independent from the state. Directors obtained the rights of owners, but the responsibilities for their enterprise were left with the state. The 1988 Law on Cooperatives also created the perfect mechanism for abuse of property: to establish cooperatives within enterprises. These cooperatives undertook the most lucrative activities for their enterprises or used the difference between the state (at the enterprise) and market (at the cooperative) prices in their favour. The difference (profits) went to the managers (they themselves, or their relatives, were the owners of the cooperatives).[19]

Spontaneous privatization is also characteristic of the right given to labour collectives to purchase rented enterprises. Stiglitz opposes rapid voucher privatization and

[19] The leadership of the USSR were fascinated with cooperatives, which they viewed as the implementation of one of Lenin's theories (see his 'On Cooperation', 1923), and adopted a special recommendation to create cooperatives within state enterprises. By the time they realized what this meant, it was too late.

prefers a solid, moderately paced mechanism to transfer lease-based enterprises (those that are to be rented with a right to purchase, or lease-with-purchase deals). Furthermore, as an example of Gorbachev's institutional incremental system, he points to renting with a right to purchase. According to Stiglitz (1999, p. 25), so-called reformers (his expression) should have adhered to this model. But it is well known in Russia that one of the arguments which led to rapid voucher privatization was the spread of the lease-with-purchase system. In the vast majority of cases this system served as an instrument for managers to obtain the property of their enterprises for free.

The reality was very different from the way the critics saw it. Accelerated privatization in Russia was not a mechanism to take the state out of the economy, but an attempt by the state to catch the last coach of a departing train named socialist property. The privatization programme, though it had its own problems, facilitated the restoration of some measure of property management and brought some order to society.

Without taking into account the initial lack of real mechanisms of state control over property, the apparent contradictions in Stiglitz's paper are unavoidable. On the one hand, he asserts that control over directors of state enterprises could be considered as an alternative to an accelerated privatization (p. 10). On the other hand, it is clear that the state is unable to regulate the activities of the funds' managers efficiently (p. 12). In the first case we are talking about hundreds of thousands of enterprises in a collapsing state (at the beginning of the 1990s) and in the second case we are only discussing several dozen funds.

Finally, Stiglitz recommends undertaking privatization in favour of the stakeholders and applying the principles of businesses managed by an owner or a family firm to medium and large companies (p. 13). What he is recommending is privatization in favour of an enterprise's employees. According to Stiglitz, they 'are not unrelated absentee shareholders who see the enterprise only as a "property" (perhaps to be quickly harvested)' (p. 14). Such theories, however, are based on a limited knowledge of both the Russian privatization experience and the functioning of Russian companies. First and foremost, the great majority of Russian enterprises had been privatized in favour of labour collectives, which hardly facilitated the transformation of the latter into the hands of efficient owners. On the contrary, privatization in favour of employees helped directors to obtain full control over their enterprises; in fact, this was the case from the very beginning, when there were threats of sackings (if voting did not go their way), and later, when employees sold their shares voluntarily or under duress. As a result, the proposed privatization mechanism facilitates the process of 'asset stripping and looting that leads to the demise of an enterprise' (p. 13). There is no evidence here that privatization in favour of stakeholders is capable of showing better results.[20]

[20] I have not discussed the fairness of this type of privatization mechanism, which puts those closer to better assets in a more favourable and advantageous position to participate in privatization. Nevertheless, this argument is rather important, because we are not talking about a one-off privatization, but the reallocation of property in a country where the whole population has been deprived of it.

The roots of the reformers' errors: the professors' approach

Another set of criticisms directed at Russian reformers targets the various sources of their mistakes and the errors that underlie the defects in Russia's economic policy during the last decade. This perception of Russian reformers' mistakes reveals the roots of many misunderstandings and confusions – misunderstandings that are unusual for serious economists.

The theoretical and ideological preferences of those who led the government at the beginning of the reforms are often considered to be the main reason behind their poor results. The following issues, according to critics, contributed to the lack of success of the Russian economic reforms of 1990s.

● First and foremost, the reformers are accused of being fascinated with theoretical models from textbooks, and those textbooks are condemned as not of the best quality. Stiglitz is adamant that the reasons for the Russian reforms' failure is 'a failure to understand what makes an actual market economy function – a failure arising in part from the neoclassical model itself'. He suggests that the reformers 'were overly influenced by the excessively simplistic textbook models of the market economy' (Stiglitz, 1999, p. 4).

● Second, the ideological prejudice of the reformers, along with their wish to close the communist past and its inherited institutions, determined their desire to demolish those institutions rapidly and without an immediate substitute. But as the Chinese experience also proves, poor existing institutions are better than none at all.

- The third reason for those mistakes was, apparently, inadequate advice from foreign experts (mostly American, as west European critics like to stress) who were actively working with the Russian government during the first post-communist years. Their role is usually considered to be the reason for such defects in the Russian model as shock therapy and excessive attention to macroeconomics, privatization and strict monetary stabilization. According to Brovkin, 'No one can dispute that shock therapy was a western product imposed on Russia by western advisers and their Russian students' (Brovkin, 1999, p. 22). This thesis is asserted by almost any solid Sovietologist paper.

- Fourth, there is criticism of international financial institutions, which imposed inadequate reforms on Russia and provided bad advice. This criticism is based upon the 'Washington consensus'.[21]

- Finally, the 'vicious' character of the 1990s in Russia (as imposed by the West, the IMF, etc.) is explained by the lack of understanding of the historical, cultural and national traditions of this country, with its glamorous past and heroic present. Knowledge of Russian and especially Soviet history is perceived as

[21] There is another position – that international financial institutions did not provide Russian reformers with assistance when the Russian reformers still had political capital to undertake major market reforms. See Sachs (1996), pp. 128–33; Åslund (1999). It is not within the scope of this paper to discuss this issue.

the key to understanding how to reform the economy. Sovietology, according to this logic, becomes the main trustee and source of wisdom for a post-communist country. Researchers with a strong background in the Soviet economy should be looked upon as genuine experts.[22] These include Sovietologists who were completely unable to assess the real contradictions of a Soviet system and to forecast its development within Gorbachev's perestroika. That is why they were offended by Russian reforms. Most of them did not understand, and do not want to understand, the real problems and the logic of a post-communist economy.

All of these views are closely intertwined. They are all based on a misguided approach to economic policy decision-making. They include the idea that an economic policy is the result of a plan worked out in an academic setting; the belief that there are correct and incorrect economic theories; the perception that an economic theory directly influences market behaviour; and the belief that economic advisers must give advice, and politicians must implement this advice.

When critics say that it is impossible to develop an economic policy based on certain textbooks and theories, they immediately offer other textbooks and theories. From this perspective, all the reform failures appear to be caused by the fact that the work of Keynes,

[22] It is revealing that Stiglitz refers to the paper of M. Weitzman, 'who, unlike the most prominent western advisors, was a scholar of Soviet-style economies'; that is why he 'gave the pragmatic argument …' (see Stiglitz, 1999, p. 14, footnote 26). One could quote Stalin, who possessed colossal experience in this area, on the same grounds.

Schumpeter and Hayek was ignored. The textbooks on economic theory that focus on information economics instead of a 'genuine' neo-classical approach were not appreciated enough either; the reformers used 'the typical American style textbook [which] relies so heavily on a particular intellectual tradition, the neoclassical model, leaving out other traditions' (Stiglitz, 1999, p. 3). Certainly, when theoreticians criticize practical politicians, different authors blame the latter for their sins, although their conclusions are the same. For example, Stiglitz reproaches Russian reformers for not paying enough attention to Hayek's approach, whereas many Russian critics consider the fascination with Hayek to be the reason for the failures of reform.

The naïve belief in economic advice and advisers' power is also rather strange. We are not discussing the issue of which Western advisers were involved in actual economic and political decisions. There were many self-proclaimed advisers to the Russian government or the president who only once met one of many deputy ministers (there have been many more deputy ministers in Russia than, say, in Great Britain or in the United States).[23]

[23] Michael McFaul gives an excellent description of the role of many Western advisors and of understanding of this role in the West: 'It is silly when a commentator or columnist blames the Clinton administration for Russian lawlessness, economic depression, or the Chechen war. It is equally silly when a consultant from the U.S. Agency for International Development (USAID) claims that the United States privatized 100,000 Russian enterprises; when an American professor returns home triumphantly to declare that he rewrote the Russian constitution; or when *Time* magazine devotes its cover to celebrating how three U.S. campaign consultants orchestrated Yeltsin's 1996 re-election comeback' (McFaul, 1999, pp. 60–61).

More important, the role of an economic adviser never includes, and should not include, political decisions. Decision-making is the responsibility of politicians and administrators. An adviser should analyse the situation from a theoretical and historical point of view that includes his or her own experience. Another question is how good or bad such an arrangement is. It is both fair and appropriate that politicians or public servants (who are responsible to the voters or to their own bosses) take political decisions.

The limited sphere of economic advisers' professional knowledge makes them both weak and strong. Politicians, when making a decision, possess more facts than economic policy advisers, including a knowledge of the real balance of social forces, interest groups and concrete (often short-lived) political objectives. As a result they cannot rely simply on theoretical and historical concepts. If an economist does not appreciate his or her role as an adviser, it can lead to conflicts and misunderstandings.

Politicians accept recommendations from advisers under two circumstances. First, advisers' suggestions are accepted if they are obvious; for example, the necessity for budget equilibrium, price liberalization, fighting hyperinflation. Of course, sometimes there are recommendations not to balance the budget, not to stop inflation, etc, but these arguments are too exotic for serious economic discussion. Anyone who remembers empty stores in the autumn of 1991 and the real threat of hunger in Russian cities understands why the prices were liberalized without any prolonged discussions.

25

Second, politicians will accept recommendations that correlate with a developing balance of political and economic forces. 'Politics is the art of the possible', as Gorbachev like to repeat.

These two factors determine a politician's choice of advisers. During the last decade, there have been many advisers in Moscow. They proposed various ways to save the country, and their recommendations often radically contradict one another.

Anyone who has dealt with the practical development and implementation of an economic policy is well aware that all advisers play a relatively small role, even in stable democracies. The problems highlighted above are even more complicated in a transition economy that lacks institutional stability and a consensus on basic social values.

Similar issues arise with the programmes of international financial institutions (particularly the IMF). The criticism of our Western colleagues is contradictory: on the one hand, projects agreed upon with the IMF are described as not implemented or poorly implemented; on the other hand, the same projects are described as mistaken. There are again two approaches to the same problem: a general economic one and a technical economic one.

The general point of view deals with the 'Washington consensus' concept which is criticized for its lack of attention to institutional aspects of transition. Institutional reforms take decades, and there is an immediate need to balance the market and the budget and to stabilize the currency. Therefore, it is practically impossible to solve these two problems simultaneously. It is possible only from a theoretical point of view. Very few politicians (except for dictators) are able to undertake institutional reforms during a severe financial crisis.

Arguments about the role of foreign advisers can also be applied to the more technical issues related to governmental agreements with the IMF and the World Bank. But there is one additional circumstance that is rarely taken into an account. A good number of IMF conditionalities were developed in Moscow, not in Washington. Russian politicians are the ones who initiated many of these conditions. And only then were they 'imposed from the outside' – 'from Washington' – and this is quite a typical way for a weak government to launch unpopular reforms.

Similar arguments can be applied to the 'ideological prejudice' of the reformers. In order to implement an ideology, there should be corresponding social forces (groups of interests) which are ready to support this ideology. A politician's decision is significant for stable societies. Post-communist Russia exhibited a highly turbulent socio-economic structure hampered by the weak role of both private and state institutions. The ideological priorities of the reformers were not as clear as they seemed initially. They chose the liberal strategy of transformation, but to a great extent their choice was predetermined by an economic system whose development was characteristic of the end of the 20th century. Yet the practical steps taken by the reformers make the arguments of 'ideological prejudice' even less coherent. In the privatization programme, the voucher mechanism did not correspond to the reformers' theories, but it was in line with the logic of crisis. The same is true for a great number of other government decisions during the 1990s.

The theoretical approach suffers from a further problem. The cultural, historical and geographical peculiarities of the country can be used to explain anything. For instance, the Russian Development Bank was described as a necessity because of the size of the country and its ten time zones; non-payments and barter transactions were also put down to Russia's huge territory; the multiplicity of currency rates, meanwhile, was reportedly the result of the peculiarities of the national character. The list is endless. I would suggest that reference to a country's national–historical–cultural peculiarities is used at best when there are no other arguments to explain a problem, or – at worst – when one wants to steal something.

National and cultural peculiarities cannot be quantified. The same historical arguments can prove thesis and antithesis: that Russia is the most individualistic or the most collectivist of countries, that liberalism is a historically foreign concept for Russia or perfectly suited to the country, and so on. It sometimes seems that the national–cultural–historical explanation plays the same role as the *deus ex machina* of Greek tragedy: it appears when there are no other arguments. (This is true not only for Russia: for 15 years after the Second World War, researchers viewed Japan's economic policy with great scepticism because of 'Japanese traditions and national character'. Later, the same arguments were used to explain 'the Japanese economic miracle'.)

Nevertheless, there is one important factor connected with the country's peculiarities. This is the level of economic development measured as GNP per capita. I have already stressed this factor while comparing reforms in Russia and China. However, its implications are much greater. Many national differences which seem acute become much milder (or even disappear) when different countries are considered at comparable stages of their socio-economic development.

Finally, if the problem rests with the wrong textbooks, advisers and ideology, why have all Russian governments during the 1990s pursued the same policy with similar basic elements? These governments were different both politically and intellectually. Their understanding of the country's historical experience and traditions was dramatically different. 'Monetarist' Yegor Gaidar was replaced by 'strict administrator' Viktor Chernomyrdin who was the great hope of all the lobbyists and communists. But he continued (if inconsistently) the policy of stabilizing the macroeconomic situation,[24] and voucher privatization was implemented. The same direction was taken by the 'young reformer' Sergei Kiriyenko. 'Heavyweight' Yevgenii Primakov brought a lot of hope to the left wing, whose representatives played a major role in his government, and was supported by a left-wing and nationalist majority of the state Duma. Nevertheless, Primakov also chose a policy of tough macroeconomic stabilization. Sergei Stepashin and Vladimir Putin chose the same path. Why was this? I believe there

[24] Not long before his resignation, at the beginning of 1998, Chernomyrdin even spoke of the victory of 'our right monetary policy' during an open meeting of the government.

29

are deep-rooted factors that made all these prime ministers, with some variations, pursue the same direction.

The characteristic feature of all of the criticisms directed at Russian reform that I have listed is their attention to theoretical models at the expense of practical ones. Not only has the approach been too abstract, there has also been a refusal to analyse events. Most recommendations deal with a desirable policy, and not with practical issues and constraints. They portray a lack of in-depth knowledge of the Russian experience. This lack can be seen in the sources chosen by some ill-informed Western experts for their research: there is an excess of theoretical and Sovietologist papers and a dearth of studies written by economists directly involved in implementing Russian reforms.[25]

Discussion of the reasons for the failure of market reforms has been reduced to a choice between the wrong set of reforms or a good set of reforms implemented in an inconsistent manner (Stiglitz, 1999, p. 3). I believe, however, that the problem is much more complicated than that. Setting aside personal issues and agendas, one should be able to distinguish the policy being *implemented* (not just discussed).

In this case, criticism related to historical, national and cultural peculiarities should not neglect the real features of the Russian reforms compared with those of

[25] Academics were also involved in a practical policy which became a special feature of the post-communist reforms. In a more 'normal' development, only professional politicians and administrators would have enjoyed such a high level of involvement. J.Williamson was one of the first to notice this (see Williamson, 1994).

other post-communist countries. Here, the path of reforms is more complicated, with many more contradictions and conflicts than have occurred in most central and east European countries.

3   THE POST-COMMUNIST TRANSFORMATION IN RUSSIA AS A SPECIAL CASE

'Why were the reformers so unwilling to start from where they were?', Stiglitz asks (Stiglitz, 1999, p. 24). He does not really answer the question (he sees the reason as that the reformers *did not want* to start from where they were). But the problem is quite different: the reformers had to start from exactly where they were – the situation was predetermined by circumstances in the autumn of 1991, when the first Russian post-communist government was created.

The weak state and the revolution

The fundamental feature of Russian post-communist reforms is that they were implemented at a time of weak state power. Critics of Russian reforms often ignore this fact or view it as a result of the reformers' deliberate activities. For them, the reformers' liberal and anti-communist ideology is the reason for the rapid liberalization and privatization that led to the crisis in state power. The real process, however, was quite different.

A radical (systemic) social transformation under a weak state government is, in essence, the definition of revolution. This is a principal consideration in the comparison of the modern Russian transformation with that of other post-communist countries. Russia is the only country (except for China) which developed its own communist system. Consequently, the exit from communism is a much more complicated task than for those countries that had communism imposed upon them from outside. It involves breaking a national consensus and causing frictions between various social forces and interest groups. For central and eastern Europe overcoming the communist past and joining European society is an objective that unites their peoples. In the case of Russia, however, moving the country out of communism and the demise of the empire are the sources of social tension and social disintegration.[26]

A revolutionary transformation has its own logic and stages of development, including economic ones (i.e. the special features of an economic policy and the dynamics of the business processes).[27] An economic policy in a society torn apart by social struggle cannot be stable and consistent. First and foremost, social chaos is reflected in the state's inability to influence social and economic processes. This weakness needs to be incorporated into any discussion of modern Russian economic development. No researcher should ignore this fact.

The state's weakness is reflected in the volatility of economic policy and trends, in the multiple centres of power competing with one another, and in the lack of sustainable, stable political institutions and of any

[26] For the detailed argument relating to the revolutionary character of the Russian transformation, see Mau and Starodubrovskaya (1999). There is also a justification for 'a revolutionary economic crisis' phenomenon. Among Western researchers see McFaul (1990); McFaul (1997); and Goldstone (1991).
[27] Brinton (1965) discusses these stages of development in more detail.

33

acceptable, consistent 'rules of play'. A state's weakness also causes a number of special economic problems. This is evident not only in the experiences of modern Russian, but also in those of the great revolutions of the past (this topic is largely beyond the scope of this paper).[28]

Important economic consequences of a transformation under a weak government include:

- an inability to collect taxes, which leads to an inflation tax increase and/or aggravates a budget crisis. As a result, the state is heavily under-budgeted and the government is unable to pay its bills. (I would like to stress that this is typical for almost all countries.)

- a rapid increase in transaction costs. This decreases domestic production competitiveness.

- the demonetization of the national economy. (This also happened in countries where inflation of paper money was avoided because of metal coinage, but cash was converted into treasury bills.)

- the state's weakness makes an unavoidable impact on privatization by promoting socio-political objectives (to stabilize power) or fiscal ones.

A weak state is extremely vulnerable to corruption and pressures by lobby groups. In Russia's case, it is impossible to strengthen state power by expanding the rights of the government to interfere in the economy. One often hears that the Russian state is corrupt, that the

[28] For example, see Ashley (1962); Aflation (1990); and Mau and Starodubrovskaya (1999).

Russian state is weak and that one should empower the state; in other words, expand the power of a corrupted state. Of course, Russia must strengthen its government. However, such an objective should not just expand the government's ability to interfere in the economy, especially to allocate rare raw materials (material or financial) at its own discretion. (Naturally, this is 'for the benefit of the nation' as any Russian *dirigiste* will tell you!)

These facts reveal the most important feature of a weak government approach to development and the implementation of economic policy. The quest for political majority through existing political institutions (parliament, parties) that are weak, poorly structured and unstable is not as important as in stable counties. The key here is to guide the interaction between the representatives of power (the government) and the leading groups of economic interests. These groups have real political leverage and act as political parties in the early stages of transformation.[29] A. Shleifer and D. Treisman are correct when they write that 'reformers knew that any achievements of marketization would survive only if they were also able to create a powerful political coalition in support of free markets'.[30]

[29] For more detail about the role of economic agents, see Mau (1996), pp. 70–71.

[30] In their latest work Shleifer and Treisman pay special attention to the importance of another political–economic model which considers the domination of interest groups over state institutions. They write: 'In a fluid political setting, where the implementation of policies is as important and as difficult as their enactment, and where enactment relies on agreement between powerful political groups rather then a vote, elections are, at most, one of many arenas in which interest groups compete' (p. 6).

One more comment seems to be important here. A number of misinterpretations about the weakness of the Russian government and its lack of ability to provide law enforcement result from very process of creating a democratic regime, because for a democracy not only appropriate laws but experience and precedents are quite important. Many Western experts consider Russia from the USSR perspective, where the government could impose its will on society. The transition from Soviet totalitarianism to democracy appears on the surface to be a weakening of law and order, even without considering the specific problems of the revolutionary type of transformation. It is more important in a country which is longing for the creation of a modern federal system. Western students often forget that many similar problems were rather typical for a number of Western countries, and especially for the USA. 'Anyone who wonders why it is so hard for the central government to root out corruption in Russia's federal state might consider asking why it was so difficult to abolish slavery – and later segregation – in the federal United States.'[31]

Again, I would like to stress that, taken together, all the facts mentioned above are characteristic of any full-scale revolution. Analysing the modern Russian transformation from this viewpoint allows us to understand and explain many of the strange events during the last 10–15 years.

There is one complication specific to the Russian transformation: the interaction of three transformation processes instead of one. The first is a movement

[31] Treisman (1999), p. 83.

towards a market economy characteristic of all post-communist countries and China. The second is the crisis of a traditional economic industrial structure ('an economy of coal and steel') that needs to develop into a post-industrial society.[32] The third is a revolutionary economic crisis, whereby a weak state power must implement a systematic restructuring. It is this interaction of circumstances that has greatly hindered Russian reforms.

The beginning of the post-communist reforms: Jacobins, Bolsheviks and contemporary Russia

Let us return to Stiglitz's contention that Gorbachev started incremental reforms that were later destroyed by radicals.[33] This is not an accurate depiction of events.

In reality, Gorbachev's reforms (perestroika) led to an economic imbalance because of their explicitly populist character. Some experts associate such populism with simultaneous democratization. Democratization made politicians greatly dependent on public opinion. However, this does not represent the whole truth – Gorbachev's most important objective was trying to move the economy. But after some serious economic problems surfaced, Gorbachev initiated his political reforms to neutralize his opponents within the party's elite.

[32] For more detail on the crisis of a traditional industrial society as an explanation for the Russian transformation, see Rosser and Rosser (1997).

[33] According to Stiglitz (1999), p. 24, the Gorbachev-era perestroika reforms furnish a good example of incremental institutional reforms. Kots and Weir (1997) make a similar point in their discussion of the socio-political reasons which led the USSR away from 'good' Gorbachev reforms.

A number of the actions undertaken by the leadership of the USSR during the second half of the 1980s precipitated the economic and political crisis. They included an attempt to radically increase investment growth at a time of decreasing of oil prices and, consequently, budget revenue; an anti-alcohol campaign that became a significant reason for budget deficit growth; giving more power to the management of enterprises without an adequate system to hold them responsible for their economic activities; the start of spontaneous privatization (through leasing and cooperatives); an uncontrolled increase in money supply with a decreased supply of goods; and the radical liberalization of the banking system.

This type of economic policy development is characteristic of all large-scale revolutions. So-called 'moderate governments', confident in their popularity and ability to use revolutionary enthusiasm for their own goals, are prone to extravagant economic decisions. This usually aggravates an economic crisis, which then leads to further destabilization of power. The main result of perestroika's economic reform was an acute economic crisis. The following were the main elements of the crisis:

- a shortage of goods comparable only to the military economy of the 1940s or the Stalinist experiments of 1929–33;

- the beginning of economic decline and the rapid growth of the population's nominal incomes;

- the rapid evasion of taxes with a budget deficit approaching 30 per cent of GDP;

- the dramatic growth of external debt;
- the disintegration of the national economy.

In the autumn of 1991, the country was on the brink of widespread hunger that threatened to spread to the main industrial centres. *De facto*, the USSR had ceased to exist in August of that year, leaving Russia without its own currency, stable state borders, army or police. With a huge shortage of goods and the threat of food shortages, there were powerful separatist trends within Russia; its regional administrations wanted full control over 'their own' production of food and materials.[34]

One of the explanations for the beginning of post-communist reforms in Russia is that it came about as a result of bad decisions made by Boris Yeltsin and Gaidar in favour of 'monetarism' and liberal market entry. But everything that happened during 1991–2 makes such an explanation untenable. Yeltsin can hardly be viewed as a 'natural' liberal. In addition, the Russian cultural and historical traditions are not the most fertile ground for liberalism. In reality, without having proper administrative tools, the Russian government was able to do only one thing, and that was to choose a consistent path of liberalism.[35] The liberalism of 1991–2 was able to eradicate the hunger and cold of the winter, as well as mitigate the collapse of Russia.[36] However, after the real

[34] For more detail, see Gaidar (1996), pp. 132–6.
[35] This period also corresponded with a cultural and intellectual renaissance of liberalism around the world; Francis Fukuyama's article and then book, *The End of History* (1992) became a symbol of the time.
[36] There is an argument that all these dangers were exaggerated and would not have materialized. However, at the time not only

danger had passed and government administrative resources were restored, the majority of the leadership rejected economic liberalism (although they continued to apply liberal measures every time a crisis took place).

This was the birth of post-communist radicalism. However, the radicalism itself was neither a feature nor a product of the transformation revolution. As I mentioned earlier, the radicalism of the first post-communist stage is directly correlated with the depth of the macroeconomic imbalance, not the result of just one instance of political instability. A direct product of political instability would be pragmatism and an ideological freedom to take action. The latter should be discussed separately.

Stiglitz compares the radical reforms in Russia with the activities of two famous revolutionary movements of the past: the Jacobin movement and the Bolshevik movement (Stiglitz, 1999, pp. 22). There are indeed solid reasons for such a comparison, although dramatically different from the ones suggested by the author of *Whither Reform?*

In reality, there is no evidence that the rigorous and decisive actions undertaken by radical governments in the past were connected with their radical ideology, their desire to implement their objectives or their wish to break with the old regime's ways within the shortest period of time. The radical governments never stuck to their programme. It was early, 'moderate revolutionary

politicians but the population took them very seriously. Many argue that the dangers never materialized because of timely measures undertaken by the reformers.

governments' that tried to undertake a 'scientifically justified' restructuring with the best features of the old regime's experience as well as a revolution aiming at 'incremental, gradual and adaptive' changes (Brinton, 1965). In practice, the measures undertaken by the weaker power aggravated the crisis. If incremental changes did not fuel such deep crises, radical governments would never come to power. With power, radicals act pragmatically (even though their various slogans and ideological points might suggest otherwise).

From a political point of view, radical governments defend their new system from reverting to the old model. This is important: Jacobin and Bolshevik economic policies served the same idea. That is why it is easy for them to change their programmes in the process of implementation. Initially, Jacobin revolutionaries, famous for their Maximum policy, were against such actions. After their victory, the Bolsheviks undertook a particular land programme, and later rejected it. The same happened with various national ideas adopted or rejected because of the Civil War. The Bolsheviks 'rejected the money' when their military opponents (Kolchak's White Army) took over the country's gold stock.

If there is a Jacobin aspect of the first post-communist reforms in Russia, it differs from the one described by some writers. The term Jacobin does not imply an ideological commitment, the destruction of the old institutions or an accelerated restructuring. It suggests the need to concentrate all forces and resources to stabilize a political situation in order to protect a new regime from serious political and economic threats. The first post-communist Russian government recognized this necessity. It fought a threat to restore an old regime with all available means (without permitting the excesses of past revolutions). In so doing it allowed a new political system to survive, sometimes sacrificing the consistency and volatility of economic direction. Because of the flexible and decisive nature of the first post-communist Russian government, some experts have written about the political dangers in the early 1990s when they never actually materialized.[37]

Gorbachev's incremental policy (which Stiglitz agrees with) and the radical post-Gorbachev period are contradictory only on the surface. In reality, they are organically linked. The reasons are not just economic: when a major imbalance results in further painful measures to secure financial stabilization, a deep connection is formed between the experiments performed by 'moderate revolutionary reformers' and their more radical successors. This connection has been demonstrated by past revolutions and has resurfaced in modern Russia.

The weakness of state power determines almost all the economic actions of governments, above all in the way they handle privatization.

Privatization and the weak state

Stiglitz and many other critics consider voucher privatization to be the main factor which weakened the country and set in motion the other failures of the Russian economy. As we have seen, at the beginning of

[37] See, for example, Stiglitz (1999), p. 3.

privatization, state power was dramatically weakened and was unable to influence the most important public processes in the country. I would like to demonstrate how the state's weakness made an impact on privatization mechanisms and manifestations.

In general, there are three main issues to be addressed in connection with privatization: economic, fiscal and socio-political. The economic objective of privatization was to create a private owner who could run a business efficiently. The Soviet government of 1989–90 declared the same objective; it was simply afraid to call it privatization and called the process downstating. (The Soviet government was fascinated with the success of Britain's Conservative party and their prime minister, Margaret Thatcher.) However, production was declining and the country was entering an economic crisis. It was clear that decisions needed to be made. Consequently, the logical idea of democratizing the country and reorienting it towards Western values led to the acknowledgment of private property as a prerequisite for positive economic progress.

The deep fiscal crisis began in the second half of the 1980s and sparked an interest in privatization as a means of increasing the budget and decreasing the 'money burden' that resulted from the huge money supply brought to the market at the time. In reality, it was impossible to use privatization to solve the country's financial problems because for a long time there was inadequate capital and great difficulty in pricing assets.

In addition, the country's leaders wanted to utilize privatization as an instrument to strengthen their political status and create a coalition in support of this or that economic direction. This last factor became critical at the beginning of the 1990s, when the post-communist reforms entered their crucial stage, and the conflict between neo-communists and market democracy led to a number of unconstitutional excesses in 1991 and 1993. Property issues were treated as powerful arguments to unite political forces and groups of economic interests.

Something similar had happened during revolutions in other parts of the world (e.g. the English Civil War of the mid-17th century, and the French Revolution at the end of the 18th century). Property manipulation is an important feature of weak state power. Naturally, property transactions facilitate decisions in economic, fiscal and socio-political areas. However, in the short term, they often contradict one another. As a rule, the socio-political area takes precedence, followed by the fiscal area (as power is stabilized), with the economic one coming last.[38]

During the last 15 years, the objectives of privatization have gradually changed. The word privatization has been qualified according to the trends of the time – 'directors'', 'people's', and 'monetary' privatization have all appeared.

The enterprise reform of 1987–8 was intended to privatize in favour of directors. In fact, the management

[38] I must stress that I am talking about privatization with a weak state. Privatization undertaken by a stable government has a different logic. For example, the British privatization of the 1980s was able to address all three areas.

of enterprises was free from the control of any economic authorities since no owner existed apart from the state. This move by Gorbachev's administration represented one of the key revolutionary features. It was an attempt to expand the social base of the reformers, attracting directorships and labour collectives with the new right to elect directors.[39] At the same time, it destabilized the administrative and institutional structures by creating a powerful new economic group free of both administrative and market limitations.

In practice, all the normative documents regulating privatization in the Russian Federation cover economic, socio-political and fiscal areas.[40] However, there are significant differences between the documents adopted at different stages of the economic reform. Thus, the first (late Soviet) privatization documents of the Russian Federation paid more attention to political and fiscal objectives.[41] While favouring the directorship and providing labour collectives with various benefits, the Russian government strengthened its own social base in order to

[39] See Gaidar (1995), pp.149–51; and Åslund (1995), pp. 225–6.
[40] These are: decrees on property in the USSR (6 March 1990), on enterprises in the USSR (4 June 1990), on property in Russia (24 December 1990), on the privatization of state and municipal enterprises (3 June 1991), the main principles of the programme for the privatization of state and municipal enterprises in the Russian Federation for 1991 (29 December 1991); the state programme of privatization for state and municipal enterprises in the Russian Federation for 1992 (11 June 1992); the state privatization programme for state and municipal enterprises of the Russian Federation (24 December 1993).
[41] For example, see the decrees of the Russian Federation on property in Russia (24 December 1990) and on the privatization of state and municipal enterprises (3 June 1991).

balance Soviet power. Those measures were supposed to enhance the Russian government's political status both directly and indirectly (by facilitating the reporting of enterprises to the Russian Federation instead of to the Soviet Union). I must emphasize that all these measures were taken at the moderate Soviet stage of the reforms.

The first post-communist privatization documents had the following objectives: to facilitate general political and economic stabilization; to increase the productivity of enterprises' activities by transferring them into the hands of the most efficient owners; and to increase budget income.[42] There were no socio-political privatization objectives; naturally, the first government of independent Russia committed to economic liberalization expected social consequences to follow privatization. One of its main objectives was to form a class of private owners. However, it treated such an objective as strategic and did not utilize it as leverage in the battle to strengthen the new regime's political status. It changed its approach later, during the second half of 1992. Initially, the government tended to pursue the expansion of various interest groups. However, its main objective was to reach macroeconomic stabilization and overcome a fiscal crisis in the shortest period of time. The search for non-inflated sources to finance the huge state expenditures characteristic of post-socialism fostered the idea of utilizing privatization proceeds in the fuel budget.

[42] See the main principles of the privatization programme for state and municipal enterprises in the Russian Federation for 1992, approved on 29 December 1991.

However, events developed in another direction: the key socio-political issues were consolidated, and there was no strong state power. By the middle of 1992, the stabilization policy faced powerful opposition. The representatives of almost all the industries and sectors of the domestic economy united to ask for financial aid from the government. Such pressure made the government pull back from stabilization, an action that caused a rise in inflation in the autumn of 1992. At the same time, the government undertook the necessary measures to create a socio-political coalition for its support. In this respect, privatization became a key factor in the consolidation of socio-political backing.

The socio-political objectives of privatization could be implemented in two ways. The first involved attracting representatives of the directorship capable of managing their enterprises efficiently (in spite of limitations on demand and market competition) who were eager for legal property guarantees for their enterprises. The second way entailed making redistribution attractive to the population. This was the target of the mass voucher privatization model.

By the summer of 1992, the approach to privatization had changed dramatically. A fiscal objective became less important because stabilization in Russia was postponed and inflation became a stable feature that softened the budget income problem. Because of rising inflation, much less attention was paid to the efficiency of newly privatized enterprises. The socio-political objective of privatization became the dominant one. Both versions of the state privatization programme, from 11 June 1992 and particularly from 24 December 1993, demonstrate this fact.[43] Both documents stressed the importance of 'creating a deep layer of private owners as an economic base for market relations'.[44] However, in the short term, the voucher privatization mechanism had different objectives: to strengthen the role of a directorship and create a 'people's' privatization movement that would involve the country's entire population in the property redistribution process. In addition, the urban population privatized their apartments almost free of charge and the rural population privatized their land plots.

Thanks to the government's efforts in 1992–4, all the socio-political objectives were more or less attained. In 1993, the directorship was divided into supporters or opponents of the market reforms: those who became competitive in the market, and those who needed the government to provide them with constant financial support and protection in the international economic sphere. In fact, a majority of the population felt misled and declared their frustration during the parliamentary elections of 1993 and 1995. Nevertheless, the presidential elections of 1996 showed that the population had opted for the reforms.

The voucher mechanism was not efficient. The reformers themselves admitted as much. However, it was a populist move that fostered power in the short run. The voucher period facilitated the creation of new owners interested in a stable new Russian economy. It created an

[43] This was not an unusual development. It corresponds to the radical stage of revolution. For example, the French Jacobins preferred fiscal efficiency when making their decisions on land distribution.
[44] See *Privatizatsiya v Rossii* (1993), p. 70.

anti-communist and anti-inflation coalition to achieve the first macroeconomic and political stabilization objectives.

By the middle of the 1990s, with a strong new government in place and the budget crisis increasing, privatization shifted towards fiscal objectives. The government was left without an inflation tax, so it needed privatization proceeds. Such a change destabilized the previous coalition, which expected the government to continue its role of strategic partner. The government, however, was strong enough to try to stand up to the interest groups (Berezovsky, Gusinsky, etc.) that were aggravating the political struggle of 1997–8.

I am not going to discuss in detail the various privatization models of past revolutions. It is enough to say that they are surprisingly similar to modern Russian models.[45]

[45] In Mau and Starodubrovskaya (1999), the correlation between Russian privatization and the restructuring of property during past revolutions is discussed in detail. The most interesting case is the English Civil War and the various forms of property redistribution following the establishment of the republic. First, royal land was sold (most of it later appeared in the hands of parliament, Cromwell's generals and businessmen who supported them). Second, the aristocracy's land was also put up for sale (it was usually bought back by the owners, sometimes via a third party, sometimes directly). From a socio-economic point of view this was an important transaction: the treasury received additional funds, and property was freed from old feudal limitations. The English Civil War showed that the change of a property's form (from a knight's possessions to purely private property) should not be seen as identical with a change of owner. From a strategic point of view, the form is much more important. Third, the redistribution of land in Ireland was similar to the voucher system. The government did not have the funds to pay its soldiers, so it issued certificates entitling them to land in Ireland following the suppression of a revolt there. The soldiers immediately sold most of

The characteristic features of property redistribution during a revolution are as follows:

- The financial impact of property redistribution is always much smaller than expected. Sometimes, the assessments are incorrect; they can be based on old, redistributed assets. The real cost to the country is much lower because of political instability, the great volume of property to be redistributed and the necessity of expediting reforms for political purposes.

- Most of the property appears to be in the hands of intermediaries and is utilized in multiple sales. This happens because of political instability and the speed of the redistribution process. It takes an additional, sometimes rather long, period to further redistribute property in favour of an efficient owner.

- As has been proved by past revolutions, a significant part of the property is left in the hands of the established political and economic elite who can pay off a new power. This is especially true of revolutions where the political component, not the social one, predominates.

All these processes consolidate political power and strengthen the new elite. This very achievement should be treated as dominant in the process of a revolutionary transformation of property.

their certificates at a discount. For a very long time, the regime's critics blamed the government for the fact that the land appeared to be not in the hand of ordinary citizens, but in those of intermediaries. However, the Irish revolt was suppressed, and property was redistributed.

In Russia, privatization, even in its extreme forms (such as vouchers and 'loans-for-shares' deals) strengthened rather than weakened the government. Of course, one can say that the leadership was bad and inefficient. However, this is an issue of pure politics and individual opinion. From a political–economic point of view, Russian privatization should be viewed primarily as a social process that was not implementing some abstract model, but that was the result of a real political struggle between various groups of interests, some of which initially had more resources than the state itself.

4 CONCLUSION

In this paper, I have reviewed a number of the arguments made by Western critics regarding Russian reforms. This review should not be interpreted as an attempt to justify what has been done in Russia nor as a claim that there were no mistakes in the policies of the last decade. I simply wanted to illustrate that the process of Russian restructuring is a much more complicated phenomenon than it appears at first.

Similarly, the arguments put forward in this paper should not diminish a purely theoretical interest in the works written by the strict critics of the Russian reforms, nor of those written by experts who have a more positive approach to the Russian experience.[46] However, it should be clear that most of my arguments are based on articles in which Western economists disagree with one another about what is going on in Russia, and how this correlates with their own theoretical models.

---

[46] Shleifer and Treisman (forthcoming 2000) and Åslund (1999) illustrate a more positive approach, but there are few other recent examples. See Granville (forthcoming 2000) ; Hanson (1999); Szegvari (1999) ; Skidelsky and Halligan (1996).

BIBLIOGRAPHY

Abalkin, L.I., Bogomolov, O.T., Makarov, V.L. et al. (1996). 'Novaya ekonomicheskaya politika dlya Rossii: somestnoe zayavlenie rossiiskikh i amerikanskikh ekonomistov', *Nezavisimaya gazeta*, 1 July.

Aftalion, F. (1990). *The French Revolution: An Economic Interpretation* (Cambridge: Cambridge University Press).

Ashley, M. (1962). *Financial and Commercial Policy under the Cromwellian Protectorate* (London: Frank Cass).

Åslund, A. (1995). *How Russia Became a Market Economy* (Washington, DC: The Brookings Institution).

Åslund, A. (1999). 'Russia on the Mend', *Chase. International Fixed Income Research. Highlights of Current Strategy*, 7 September.

Aven, P. (1999). 'Ekonomika torga', *Kommersant*, 27 January.

Bogomolov, O. (ed.) (1996). *Reformy glazami amerikanskikh i rossiyskikh uchenykh* (Moscow: REZh).

Brinton, C. (1965). *The Anatomy of Revolution*, revised and expanded edition (New York: Vintage Books).

Brovkin, V. (1999). 'Wishful Thinking about Russia', *Transition*, June.

Dalin, S.A. (1983). *Inflyatsiya v epokhi sotsialnykh revolyutsii* (Moscow: Nauka).

Fukuyama, F. (1992). *The End of History and the Last Man* (London: Penguin Books).

Furet, F. (1996). *The French Revolution 1770–1814* (Oxford and Cambridge, Mass.: Blackwell).

Gaidar, Ye. T. (1995). *Gosudarstvo i evolutsiya* (Moscow: Yevraziya).

Gaidar, Ye. T. (1996). *Dni porazhenii i pobed* (Moscow: Vagrius).

Gaidar, Ye. T. (1997). '"Detskiye bolezni" postsotsializma (k voprosu o prirode byudzhetnogo krizisa etapa finansovoi stabilizatsii)', *Voprosy Ekonomiki*, 4.

Gaidar, Ye. T. (ed.) (1998). *Ekonomika perekhodnogo perioda: ocherki ekonomicheskoi politiki postkommunisticheskoi Rossii (1991–1998)* (Moscow: IET) (Institute for the Economy in Transition).

Goldstone, J.A. (1991). *Revolution and Rebellion in the Early Modern World* (Berkeley, CA: University of California Press).

Granville, B. (1995). *The Success of Russian Economic Reforms* (London: Royal Institute of International Affairs).

Granville, B. (forthcoming 2000). 'The Problem of Monetary Stabilization in the Russian Economy', in B. Granville and and P. Oppenheimer (eds), *Russia's Post-Communist Economy* (Oxford: Oxford University Press).

Hanson, P. (1999). 'The Russian Economic Crisis and the Future of Russian Economic Reform', *Europe–Asia Studies*, vol. 51, no. 7, November.

Illarionov, A. (1998). 'Sekret kitaiskogo ekonomicheskogo "chuda"', *Voprosy Ekonomiki*, 4.

Intrilligator, M. (1996). 'Shokiruyushchii proval "shokovoi terapii"', in O. Bogomolov (ed.), *Reformy glazami amerikanskikh i rossiyskikh uchonykh* (Moscow: REZh).

Kots, D. and Weir, F. (1997). *Revolution from above: The Demise of the Soviet System* (London and New York: Routledge).

Mau, V. (1996). *The Political History of Economic Reform in Russia, 1985–1994* (London: Centre for Research into Communist Economies).

Mau, V. (1999). *Ekonomicheskaya reforma: skvoz' prizmu konstitutsii i politiki* (Moscow: Ad Marginem).

Mau, V. and Starodubrovskaya, I. (1999). 'Economic Regularities of the Revolutionary Process', *Social Sciences*, Vol. 30, No. 1, pp. 3–19.

McFaul, M. (1990). '1789, 1917 Can Guide 1990s Soviets', *San Jose Mercury News*, 19 August.

McFaul, M. (1997). 'Revolutionary Transformations in Comparative Perspective: Defining a Post-Communist Research Agenda', in *Revolutions. Reader* (Stanford, CA: Stanford University Press).

McFaul, M. (1999). 'Getting Russia Right', *Foreign Policy*, Winter 1999–2000, No. 117, pp. 58–71.

'Milestone of Transition' (1999). *Transition*, June.

Morita, T. (1999). 'The Pretence of Market Economy and The Legacy of The Old Regime – The Political Economy of System Transformation' *Transition*, June.

Privatizatsiya v Rossii: sbornik normativnykh dokumentov i materialov Chast'1 1993. (Moscow: Yuridicheskaya literatura).

Radygin A. (1994). *Reforma sobstvennosti v Rossii: na puti iz proshlogo v budushchee* (Moscow: Respublika).

Radygin, A. (1996). *Privatisation in Russia: Hard Choices, First Results, New Targets* (London: Centre for Research into Communist Economies).

Rose, Richard (1999). 'Distributing Government Institutions, Russians Develop Survival Strategies', *Transition*, June.

Rosser, J.B. and Rosser, M.V. (1997). 'Schumpeterian Evolutionary Dynamics and the Collapse of Soviet-Bloc Socialism', *Review of Political Economy*, Vol. 9, No. 2, pp. 211–23.

Sachs, J. (1996). 'The Transition at Mid Decade', *American Economic Review Papers and Proceedings*, Vol. 86, No. 2, May.

Shleifer, A. and Treisman, D. (forthcoming 2000). *Without a Map: Political Tactics and Economic Reform in Russia.*

Sinel'nikov, S. (1995). *Byudzhetnyi krizis v Rossii: 1985–1995 gody* (Moscow: Yevraziya).

Skidelsky, R. and Halligan, L. (1996). *Macroeconomic Stabilization in Russia: Lessons of Reform, 1992–1995* (London: Social Market Foundation).

Skocpol, T. (1979). *States and Social Revolutions: A Comparative Analysis of France, Russia, and China* (Cambridge: Cambridge University Press).

Stiglitz, J. (1999). *Whither Reform? Ten Years of the Transition* (Washington, DC: The World Bank).

Szegvari, I. (1999). 'Sem'raskhozhikh tezisor o rossiiskikh reformakh: verny li oni?', *Voprosy Ekonomiki*, no. 9, pp. 45–56.

Treisman, D. (1999). 'After Yeltsin Comes ... Yeltsin', *Foreign Policy*, Winter 1999–2000, pp. 74–86.

Williamson, J. (1990). *Latin American Adjustment: How Much Has Happened?* (Washington, DC: Institute for International Economics).

Williamson, J. (1994). 'In Search of a Manual for Technopols', in Williamson J. (ed.), *The Political Economy of Policy Reform* (Washington, DC: Institute for International Economics).

World Bank (1992). *Russian Economic Reform: Crossing the Threshold of Structural Change* (Washington: The World Bank).